Acts of Witness – Stages of Worship

Communicative Drama and the plays of Charles. M. Tanner

by Lanin D. Thomasma

Acts of Witness – Stages of Worship

(Communicative Drama and the Plays of Charles M. Tanner)

TABLE OF CONTENTS

To my wife, Jean ...

... who didn't know I knew so many big words.

INTRODUCTION

This is a book about a medium of communication: Communicative Drama. It is also a book about a specific corpus of work, one which, I believe, best exemplifies and illustrates that medium. That corpus is namely the repertoire of plays written by playwright Charles M. Tanner, available and currently utilized by the Covenant Players international drama ministry.

As a clarification, I must state that I am dealing with "Communicative Drama" as a term both of effect (that which is accomplished by the dramatic work) and of intention. Obviously, any categorizing of drama works will be subjective at its best. Still, it cannot be denied that there are many dramatic pieces extant which are not written with the intent of communication. Many of the more recently written "*avant-garde*" style plays, though they may have the potential to communicate (at least to those who are sensitive to the state of mind in which they were written), still remain largely indecipherable to the majority of their audience. These plays may effect a limited communication, but their intent would seem to be more therapeutic than communicative.

Other plays are intended to communicate on a wider scale. An excellent example of the communicative potential of such plays is Arthur Miller's "THE CRUCIBLE". The play premiered at the height of the so-called "McCarthy Era", and its depiction of the Salem Witch Trials was immediately taken as a statement on Senator Joseph McCarthy's activities and that of the HUAC some years earlier. Although the playwright did intend that identification, Mr. Miller chose the setting he did to illuminate more than just the time in which he lived. Had he chosen to attack Senator McCarthy directly, his communication might have been too narrow to extend beyond that period in time. By drawing the parallel to history, Miller challenged his audience to consider the greater issues of intolerance and suspicion which served to smooth McCarthy's initial path and fuel his forward progress. Thus "THE CRUCIBLE" remains and shall remain relevant, as long as intolerance and suspicion remain a part of the human experience.

In the matter of plays specifically designed and intended to communicate, enlighten and challenge to deeper thought, there can be little doubt that, with over 3500 plays, the repertoire of plays utilized by the Covenant Players represents the most extensive and diverse array under this category. Such extent and diversity is intentional, born of the many different ways this ministry itself has been and is being utilized. The experience gained in over a million performances the world over has resulted in an unique marriage of repertoire and expertise, a body of performer/missioners trained in all aspects of communicative seed-planting.

Central to the training of this body of professionals remains, however, the plays, and to understand the plays, we must begin by understanding Communication itself...

Chapter 1

DRAMA AS COMMUNICATION

Experience as God's Educator

When we were children, we were taught by example. As we grew, those examples were translated to books, at first utilizing pictures, and then gradually segueing into words, as our reading skills increased. As our degree of comprehension grew, the terminology of the teaching became increasingly complex, but no matter how complex it may have become for us, the key to understanding almost invariably utilizes some form of the phrase "let's take an example...". Experience - ours or another's - has remained with us as our oldest and best teacher.

Personal experience provides us the deepest, most concrete teaching. In fact, most of our most ingrained fears and prejudices involve what we have personally experienced. But second in effectiveness, from the moment we master the concept of *quid pro quo*, is example, or vicarious experience. This is held by scientists to be the ultimate indication of sapience in human beings; the ability to learn a concept *without having seen it* is a sign of true intelligence.

The challenge for any mode of teaching is in the transception of the theory into action. Here, again, personal experience proves the most effective. When we burn our hand on the stove for the first time, we learn not to touch the stove again. But more amorphic concepts present difficulties, inasmuch as we can reason away any personal application of what has been learned. By translating the amorphic into the framework of our own experience or that of one close to us, we may bridge the rationale and reach the true target, the behavior patterns.

Naturally, human experts have accomplished nothing more than to identify what God has placed in Man to begin with. God, having placed this learning potential within us, uses experience as His educator in many instances throughout the Scriptures. Take for example the history of His chosen people, the Jews, and within that history, the experiences of the various Judges. In each case, God uses the span of many years, even centuries, to provide experiential teaching for His children of subsequent generations, all the more necessary since we are such slow and inadequate learners.

There are more specific examples, where men are called to demonstrate, through specific acts, the various messages of the Lord to His people. Jonah and Hosea are two such examples, Jonah unwittingly providing a prescience of the Messiah's mission; Hosea, through his choice of a wife (or, more accurately, God's choice), effectively illustrating God's willingness to reclaim Israel.

We can find even more abstract examples, such as Ezekiel's prophetic siege of Jerusalem, using a stone tablet to symbolize the city. Isaiah and Daniel both utilize symbolic accounts, or, in the case of Isaiah's song of the vineyard, popular entertainment media to communicate God's messages. The Bible abounds in the use of symbolic acts, used to illustrate every aspect of our relationship with our Heavenly Father.

Even the Lord Jesus, in His dealings with the Pharisees, brought to mind the necessity of placing the amorphics of God's Grace into visual examples: *"... so that you may know that the Son of Man has authority on earth to forgive sins ... Get up, take up your mat and go home."* (Matthew 9:6 NIV)

The point is, we are created in God's image, and so made, our creativity is the reflection of God's creative power. Because of our own finiteness, God must tailor His communication to our physical limits of sense, intellect, understanding and creativity. Vicarious experience is one of His chief tools of communication.

Drama - Applied Vicarious Experience

Psychologists have established that the combination of verbal and visual teaching increases impressively the level of comprehension. In the medium of drama, we find not only these two elements combined, but also the added element of emotional and psychological interchange; in short, we have visible experiences.

The additional advantage of drama is that, in the same manner as stories and parables, the impact of the experience is controllable, can be repeated at will. This has advantages to those who have previously seen the play presented, as well as those who view the play for the first time. The former have the opportunity to review their own reaction and to analyze the specifics of the lesson presented, while at the same time enjoying once again the experience of the play itself.

Obviously, a decisive element of this vicarious experience is empathy. Since we are creations possessing creativity, it is not necessary for us to personally experience, say, depression, in order to empathize with one who is truly depressed. Our creativity allows us to extrapolate the reactions we see, thereby making them our own. In terms of drama, this empathy leads to a process of identification between the audience and the character presented.

Properly Using the Tools

This process of identification makes it imperative that drama be utilized properly. As with any other communicative medium, there is always a danger involved. The audience allows itself to be involved in a sort of illusion, suspending their sense of reality in order to accept that the situation of the play is actually happening. Because this illusion is entered into voluntarily, a high level of trust is placed by the audience in both the playwright and the performers. In order to be true to this trust, it is the responsibility of both playwright and performer to properly use their medium.

A major clue to the proper use of drama in communication can be found in the manner in which Jesus presented His parables. Jesus rarely if ever explained the stories He told. Normally, He closed them with the challenge to "those who have ears to hear. In fact, when He did offer explanations, it was only to His disciples, those whose deeper commitment of discipleship required expanded teaching to propel their growth beyond the others around them. In this simple presentation of His teaching, Jesus presented the opportunity to those who had the wit to apply and internalize that teaching.

For the most part, very few sermons are preached throughout the Bible, the Sermon on the Mount being a very delicately-constructed exception. By the same token, we who utilize drama in communication must beware of confusing a play with a sermon, drama is most powerful when it is left open-ended. The power of interpretation, and that of choice, must be left with the audience.

The Truth in Drama

I have mentioned that drama involves a form of illusion. This has, upon occasion, led to the mistaken idea that drama does not present truth. In fact, the opposite is true. In drama, we deal with truth, but truth in essence, in heart and concept, not merely in factual occurrence. For the most part, the situations portrayed in drama are fictional, or at best conjectural. But, if we are to communicate to our audience, the reactions and histories of those fictional characters must adhere to the reality of character common to all human beings.

There are as many possible reactions to any situation as there are people. We are individual creations. But in any situation, a character's reaction must be true to that character. For example, a person of weak will cannot suddenly show great strength of will, unless that strength is, in some manner, present in his basic makeup. When such surprises take place, which indeed they may, there must be a source for the pressure which has brought such a reaction into being. A sudden change in character without a plausible explanation only diminishes that character's credibility.

The basis of any change of character must be inherent as a potential part of that character before the change takes place. We can see this in the real life example of Paul. A man visibly on fire for the Lord, Paul did not suddenly enter into his convictions. He was on fire for God while still persecuting the Church, before his conversion. The change in Paul was in the <u>direction</u> of his fire. On the other hand, Moses was gradually brought into his own. The Bible gives us a picture of Moses which is quite different than our traditional assumptions present (one example being DeMille's film, 'The Ten Commandments"). He did not immediately become a "patriarch" at the burning bush, but continued hesitating and second-guessing God's call right into the wilderness.

Both men acted true to their characters. However their situations or vocations may have changed, the basic material remained the same. Only time and God's patient hand could facilitate a change of the character's root-structure.

It is the responsibility of both playwright and performer to remain true to essential reality. Within the confines of that essential reality, however, lies an almost infinite range of possibilities (much the same as the strict metric structure of a sonnet allows an immense volume of moods, themes and expressive possibilities). To quote playwright Charles M. Tanner:

"It is a world in itself. A world with living and breathing human beings that come alive and pulsate, magnify, enlarge, explode, leap about and spiral deeply into inner cores of various kinds. The characters that you and I bring to life are truly brought to life ... They speak to us, admonish us and cause us to puzzle with them... We hurt with them and for them, we struggle in their causes, revel in their

triumphs, glory in their commitments and sigh sadly when the curtain falls ... They have become an integral part of our lives and we cannot do without them. Some we want to like, some we have a burden for, some we want to emulate, other irritate us, frustrate us, chagrin and sometimes even force us to consider in horror that they are emulating US!"

Christian Drama - a Contradiction?

Drama, as we know it today, has its origin in the Mystery, Morality and Passion plays of the Middle Ages. It was developed by the Church, an extension of the Liturgy, as a means of educating the mainly illiterate body of believers. Now, oddly enough, many branches of the Church itself are most adamant in their refusal to consider drama as a medium of Christian teaching. There have been many corruptions in the manners, methods and motivations of dramatic presentation, but when dealing with the question of whether drama can be used for Christ's work, some points must be considered.

First: can Satan drive out Satan (Mark 4:22 - 26)? We must be careful not to ascribe God's power to the devil. Satan cannot create, nor can he initiate communication that will bring a man to Christ. Satan can, however, attempt to warp what God has initiated, thus bringing it into disrepute. The example of some prominent evangelists in recent times bears witness to this, as does the ongoing debate on the type of music most suitable for worship and witness, a debate which continues to consume precious time and energy while serving no constructive purpose whatsoever.

Second: God warns us expressly against calling anything unclean that He has made clean (Acts 10:9 - 16). We would be ill-advised to summarily proclaim as unworthy of God a medium that God Himself uses in even its most abstract application (consider Chapter 4 of Ezekiel).

Third: in John Chapter 14, Jesus, who Himself told stories to illustrate His teaching, tells us that whoever has faith in Him will do even greater things through the Holy Spirit. Performing miraculous healing and preaching convicting sermons represents only a small portion of the enormous supply of gifts and talents the Lord has given His church to spread the Gospel of Jesus Christ. Our Lord has provided us with every medium of communication, and assured us that we may at all times depend upon His presence and active participation as we utilize them.

A medium of communication must be identified in the same manner as any servant of God: by its fruits. *"Jesus replied (to John the Baptist's followers), 'Go back and report to John what you hear and see: the blind receive sight, the lame walk, those who have leprosy are cured, The deaf hear, and dead are raised, and the good news is preached to the poor."* (Matthew 11:4 & 5 NIV)

The fruits of Communicative Drama lie in its effect on its audiences. Therefore, we will, throughout this book, not only be investigating the plays themselves, but we shall also review some of the reactions to performances thereof. These quotes have been gleaned from the reports of CP team leaders in various countries and languages all over the world, and cover over 40 years of Covenant Players performances. They reflect not only the depth of impact of this medium, but also the universality of its communication.

Drama is a medium, and as such, depends on its message to delineate its nature. The power of drama as Christian communication is not born of happenstance, but is direct evidence of God's Spirit at work in His vessels, to His glory, in the service of His Kingdom.

Chapter 2

ELAPSING TIME

Our lives naturally contain many memorable events, but they are not totally filled with them. Most lives are filled mainly with the 'mundane". If we were to depict every moment of a character's normal life, no matter who that character may be, we would be faced with something incredibly boring.

With few exceptions, any film, any play, any story deals in elapsed time. In films, we are able to move quickly from one pivotal event to another. In drama, that movement may be more limited. Nonetheless, both media follow the same adage: "Begin as close to the ending as possible." In other words, include only such information as is required to adequately tell the story, and no more. This is one of the elements that make drama such a communicative tool. For through drama we are given the chance to see not only the outset of an endeavor, but also its end.

The play "WHERE THE HEART IS" by Charles M. Tanner presents such a view of the Church, by means of an allegory. The play depicts a small lifesaving station, run by six men. The "leader" of these men is Paul, a man whose whole being is given to the task of locating and rescuing shipwrecked sailors.

All this changes when the lifesaving team is presented with an award by the city for their work. Suddenly, Paul and his co-worker, Silas, are met by one of the major figures in the community, Simon. Simon is full of ideas on how to publicize the team, raise money and improve the overall equipment and operation. Along with Simon is Helen, whose ideas go far beyond the practical equipping of the lifesaving team. Helen wishes to establish a support organization and build a new facility to house it. The two, intent on their projects, almost forget Paul and Silas completely - other than to name Paul as Honorary President of the group.

The scene shifts, and we move ahead five years, finding ourselves in a modern, beautifully-furnished "clubhouse". The only item that recalls the original purpose of this "club" is a polished, gilded lifesaving ring on the wall - and it appears that its days as a decoration are numbered as well. The lifesaving team still exists - in its original strength of six people. The other members (some 800 in all) are involved in various social functions. Most of the male members of the club, in fact, have never been in a boat at all.

In the midst of a committee meeting, news comes to the members of a shipwreck just off the coast. The lifesaving crew has already been mobilized, and the first survivors are being brought in. The committee is shocked to hear that it was a coal ship that sank - and that the crewmembers are Chinese! Helen, at the head of the committee, presses Simon to forbid the crew from bringing any of the survivors into the clubhouse.

When Paul receives Simon's order, he quickly squares off with Simon, insisting that the men receive warmth, shelter and proper care. Simon gives Paul and Silas an ultimatum: either they abide by the club's decision or they leave:

Simon And let me remind you two that you're not club members. You chose of your own free will to stay on the professional team. You take orders from us and we say those dirty, soaking hulks don't come in here.

Paul (Looks as though he would strike Simon, calms down) All right, Simon. We'll take them to the garage. Send the blankets and food as you promised. They've got to have it.

Silas Why don't we bring them in, anyway? Don't let this windbag stop us.

Paul Silas, we must still think of those people. Taking them into the middle of a fight won't help them. We, especially now, must not lose sight of the goal.

Silas You make sense, as always. Blast it! But I'm quitting this outfit, the moment we get all the people in from this wreck.

Paul Yes. We must both do that, Silas. We shall move down the coast a ways and start again. The job has to be done.

Silas And it's obvious it can't be done here.

Simon It's just as well. Some of the members had begun to

complain about you. Frankly, you lower the prestige of our club.

Here we have the entire history of the development of the Christian Church in one simple, powerful package. This play, written in 1962, actually predates the inception of Covenant Players. Since its premiere performance, it has literally become enmeshed in the fabric of the Church's history. Recently, in fact, I found a précis of the play related as part of the course for new members at a large church. In all likelihood, whoever had written the account was unaware of its origin; perhaps he had heard the story from a second-hand, or even a third-hand, account of someone who had viewed the play. Still, the power of the analogy was strong enough to inspire its use, once again and in another form, as a teaching tool.

Its strength is also reflected in the personal reactions that have been expressed whenever the play has been performed:

"I don't know if that was entertainment or indictment."

"I liked the one about the lifesaving station best. It had the strongest message. It spoke the most powerfully to us, about what we are going through."

"I think it tells the story of the church; we started out with good intentions and then got so big in size that we got wrapped up in the social events - and that's all we go to. So we forget about the saving of lives, which is what we are here for. Your message was very clear and I thank you for that."

"That really touched my heart. We can really get trapped in that, can't we, so easily. We really can."

Using elapsed time in communicative drama helps us hone our own analytical skills. The more we consider the consequences that come from the actions of those we view onstage, the more equipped we become to consider those of our own actions. "WHERE THE HEART IS" does not provide for us a happy, satisfying reconciliation to the conflict between Paul and Silas and the 'Lifesaving Club".

Rather, it presents a true and faithful view of just how incompatible is the path of dedicated service to Christ with that of complacence and self-indulgence.

Chapter 3

REACHING BEYOND THE CHRISTIAN CIRCLE

C. S. Lewis, in his book, "Mere Christianity", identifies an element in Man that is attuned to spiritual things, things beyond the realm of physical experience. He writes that even as children, we are able to identify, beyond the simple identification of "pleasurable" or "not pleasurable", what is "right" and "wrong", "fair" or "unfair".

This spiritual element of our being, far from being abstract, is a very concrete factor in our determinations. In fact, our discernment of such aspects as quality, integrity, fairness, ethical behavior, will often lead us to decisions which are directly at odds with our "feelings", our wants or desires, (our "druthers", to quote Al Capp). We may, to appease our desires, eventually succeed in squelching our spiritual element into silence, but we cannot dispose of it. We remain, as Lewis describes in "The Screwtape Letters", spiritual amphibians: part animal, part spirit, inexorably tied to both.

The Spiritual Element

Curiously, this spiritual element has often been ignored, particularly in recent times, by both actors and playwrights. It is natural for one who would ignore God to ignore the Spirit, but it is hard to do so without sacrificing credibility. This can be seen, for example, in the popular "Indiana Jones" films. After having been brought into a direct experience with the reality of the power of God in the climax of the first film, we find that, spiritually, Indiana Jones has not changed in the slightest. Even if it would be too much to expect a complete conversion of him, a heightened interest in the God of the Ark, who has manifest Himself so strongly, would at least be anticipated. The fact that nothing of the kind can be seen may not diminish the film's entertainment value, but it does relegate the situation to fantasy.

Such direct encounters with God are rare in today's media. The spiritual element covers a much wider scope, however. Is it necessary to deal directly with God when dealing with spiritual values? No. In fact, there are situations that demand that we focus on the spirit without mentioning God. We can see that, at times, the merest mention of "religious" terminology can close off communication (the rapidly polarizing atmosphere of the American school system exemplifies this). If we are to discuss values in terms of absolutes with those who do not accept the source of those absolutes, we must find a way to do so outside the realm of Christian verbiage. Once again, our Lord has provided us with examples of how this can be done. Jesus' parables were designed to speak clearly to both the "spiritual" and the "unspiritual". The parable of the Good Samaritan, for example, can be told completely in terms of temporal experience, without diminishing in the slightest degree the innate lesson of Man's responsibility to God for his fellow Man. Often, in fact, those less spiritually attuned were the quicker to catch the common sense of what Jesus taught. His purpose was to take us out of our normal thinking patterns.

Parables for Today

Jesus' parables were taken from the everyday lives of the people to whom He spoke. The more we understand the cultural conditions of His time, the more we can see the truth reflected in the stories He told.

Today, dramatic expression provides us with a wide range of possibilities for our modem-day "parables". Allegorical plays use a delicate balance of the concrete and the symbolic. We have seen already how the events and persons of history can be used in communication. The same holds true for today's events.

For example, the actions of such sports personalities as Steve Garvey, and, in more recent times, Steve Largent, both of whom, in their own way, resisted the popular tendency to break their contracts for the sake of higher settlements, provide the basis for Charles Tanner's play, "TRUST". The protagonist, Chip, a young but proficient athlete, is teased by a classmate for being the "Steve Largent of the school".

Chip (A sharp look) Steve Largent? What's he have to do with me?

Harry (Waves) Aw man, you know. He's the 'good' guy of the big leagues and all that stuff.

Chip (Shakes is head) You know, it's hard to believe but you set that up as a sneer. The way you said good guy. You made a face - as though being a good guy was something - what? Degrading, disgusting, a chronic disease.

Harry's comment evokes a strong response from Chip, who has become weary of the cheapness of those around him, the willingness to sacrifice integrity for money. Chip, in trying to make his friend see the value of trust, cites various situations in which trust is intrinsic to our everyday lives:

Chip Harry, you're a prospector. Out in the hills your old geiger counter and you have uncovered a mother-lode of uranium ore. It's in land-grant area so all you gotta do is... put in your claim... Suddenly, this other prospector comes up and sees what you've found. You gotta dash, so you stake your claim and ask the guy to watch things for you. (A pause) Who'd you like the guy to be? Largent or a contract-breaker?

The point is trust, Harry. You giggle and sneer at trust - and trustworthiness - but you depend upon it every day of your life. You need a lot of other people being trustworthy simply in order to say alive. Try riding an elevator just repaired by a mechanic you wouldn't trust winding up a toy duck?

Every time you take a plane to the East, to San Francisco, Hawaii, wherever, you put total trust in the designers of the airplane, the pilots, the radio man, the engineers...

What does it take to get through to you? To communicate that without trust we are not only in a mess all around but that we may be in actual danger or are stopped from doing anything.

Through plays of this and similar natures, spiritual values and conflicts can be addressed without using language and tones that might be pounced upon by those so inclined as being "religious" in nature. It is due to this that Covenant Players has been able, and is still able, to work effectively in school settings where overt reference to Christianity is not allowed. Their unique approach has taken them to schools not only in all parts of the United States, but also in Scandinavia (which applies a similar separation of the ecclesiastic and the academic), and even the People's Republic of China.

Reactions from students in all of these areas reflect the universal effect of drama applied in this manner:

"That one in the gym ("Trust") was right on!"

"You know, that "TRUST" thing with the two guys was real. It showed the frustration of (communication) and how they come together in the end."

"It is hard to keep the attention of the audience with plays that deal so completely with moral issues, but you executed it well."

"You lived up to everything your brochure said and beyond. Spellbound! The kids were spellbound! Especially the eighth graders - and they rarely have their mouths shut!"

Similar approaches can be taken on any portion of the spiritual element. Faith (itself a close cousin to Trust), Selflessness, Graciousness, Vision, Positivity, Self-control; every evidence of the spiritual element has its application in our everyday life, and in the dramatic reflection of that life. It is an intrinsic part of the whole of Man - and it is to the whole of Man that God, through us, reaches out.

Chapter 4

APPROACHES TO DAILY WITNESS

Having now whetted the appetite for spiritual qualities, we now have provided the framework for the vital next step. Such concepts as integrity, trust, compassion, purpose or quality have little meaning without the existence of an absolute standard of measurement.

Those who would deny God often overlook this fact. Without God, there is no reason to act with integrity. We should much rather fight for all we can in this life, if this life is all that we have. If we are not created for a purpose, there is no reason to seek purpose as a virtue in itself.

On the other hand, even though we may deny the Author of the virtues we seek, the very search on which we have placed ourselves places us closer to God than we may allow ourselves to be aware. There are many people around us, in fact, who are unknowingly or unadmittingly, just as close to Christ as the consciously committed Christian. For these individuals, we who know Him have the potential to be catalysts, to provide the impetus to their fulfillment, by listening to the Spirit and living our witness to Him.

Beacons to the Open Hearts

Communicative Drama can provide us with instructive case-examples of how this can be done, such as the Charles M. Tanner play, "CHRISTMAS EVE".

Here we see a young woman, Gina, who, on the way home for the Christmas holidays, finds herself stranded at the airport. It being Christmas Eve, the airport is virtually empty, but for one man, Bob, who has missed his flight (on purpose, in response to an unidentified urging, as he later discloses). Gina seems distracted, depressed beyond the simple frustration of being delayed (in fact, the delay appears to be of little concern to her at all), but not so much so that she does not hear Bob comment, half to himself, that Christmas Eve is "the loneliest night of the year".

Gina, who has herself been entertaining similar thoughts, nevertheless cannot resist taking polite exception to Bob's words, and the two embark almost unwillingly in conversation, about Christmas, and their own reasons for not adhering to or exhibiting the characteristic "holiday cheer". Bob finds himself, in the course of the conversation, becoming interested less in Gina as a woman, than in her deep feeling and understanding of Christmas itself.

Her parents having died when she was young, Gina lived with her grandparents. They have also passed away recently, leaving her with no close family, and no one with a feeling for what she has come to see in Christmas; "the throbbing pulse of hope and promise - the blessed excitement of its fullest meaning".

Bob's fascination with Gina's depth of understanding stems, he finds, from the fact that his own experience is so diametrically opposed to hers. His parents being wealthy socialites, he has spent his holidays as a child with various governesses, none of whom laid much store in the meanings of Christmas. He received many gifts, but little love. He is, therefore, drawn to Gina's fervor of feeling. Sensing this, Gina gently reveals the source of that fervor: Jesus the Christ.

Bob is at first taken aback at the fact that Gina is a Christian, but soon realizes that that is merely the reflection of his own stereotypes of "religious" people, engendered mainly by the atmosphere of his surroundings, such as the publishing house where he has, up to now, been employed ("one of the modern variety", in Bob's own words, "Down with everything and up with nothing.").

Bob — I guess that was a dumb statement, wasn't it?

Gina — Very dumb.

Bob — I'm sorry. I apologize most profusely.

Gina — You'd better apologize to all Christians. There are many who are truly beautiful, hordes who are handsome or pretty, all are attractive in some manner, and some are even - talented.

Bob — Shall I do penance?

Gina — We don't believe in it. Let's celebrate instead.

Gina's idea is to have their own Christmas celebration, using whatever they can find nearby for decorations, and making gifts for one another out of whatever they may have.

Bob You'll have to help me along the way. I've never experienced a real Christmas before.

Gina Perhaps I haven't either. But we most certainly will this night.

Bob Well, I'll get the candy and gum and stuff.

Gina First things first.

Bob What?

Gina We should read the Christmas Story. That IS the real reason for all our hope, all our chances, all our promise and all our celebration.

Here we have a challenge similar to that faced by Charles Schultz and the producers of the first 'Peanuts" television special, "A Charlie Brown Christmas". Normal audiences, say the logical minds of the experts, will not sit still long enough to hear eight to ten minutes of Bible readings. The very idea that the reading is taken from the Bible should be enough to close off the minds of many viewers.

But in "CHRISTMAS EVE", given the proper context, the individual identification with someone who truly wishes to hear the words of the Bible and is prepared to listen to them with concentration, the audience chooses instead to concentrate along with him. Experience proves this. No matter whether the audience is an average church congregation, a group of kindergarten children, the inmates of a maximum-security prison, or visitors to an inner-city mission, the reading of the Christmas story in "CHRISTMAS EVE" has, without variation, been received with total silence and rapt attention on the part of the audience. And the overall reaction to the play has always been one of strong conviction:

"I just don't have the words for that one in the airport. I felt like I was in that seat with you. I was in that position a few years ago."

"When the play was going on, you could hear a pin drop. We were all listening so intently. Every word had meaning. There was nothing wasted. Congratulations to you and your playwright."

"My husband and I both cried. He hasn't had a lot of experience with theater, but he said that was the best thing he's ever seen. So many people could identify with specific things in the program. I know he really identified with the loneliness aspect - he's really felt that with his deafness."

"I worked in the Army as a medical assistant (during WWII). I usually wound up working on Christmas Eve and on Christmas. It was really sad to meet some the GIs that couldn't go home because of illness or wounds. I remember all too often that I was in someone's room just to cheer them up a bit. It's so important to minister to those people, and you've proved that today."

"My husband is a non-believer. If tonight didn't get through to him, I don't know what will."

"That was the best Christmas message I have ever heard. And I'm almost 82, and was an ordained minister in the Methodist Church for over 40 years, so you know it was powerful!"

"That was so... I can't find the right word. I don't think there is one. Thank you is just too inadequate. It was beautiful. You have brought this old man to tears (he was indeed crying at this point). You have touched me so deeply tonight. It is a tremendous gift you are giving to everyone you serve. The one you did about Christmas Eve really struck a chord for me. It spoke to me of the rent I have to pay for being here. I must look outside me and see the needs of others. (More tears at this point) You know, I haven't cried since my wife passed on, and just like that young girl, I have been living my loss and not her gain. Because of you, I won't any more. (Then, looking up, he added) I promise you, God."

"CHRISTMAS EVE" is a play that has often been performed throughout the year, not only at the Christmas season. This is due to the very universality of its theme. As Gina reads the story of the baby Jesus, we find ourselves listening as raptly as Bob does, and, along with Gina, we remember that we each have the opportunity to reach out to those near to us, not only to those we see, but to those who see us as well.

Chapter 5

LEARNING BY TEACHING

The process of reaching out brings with it an interesting effect: as we share our faith, we find it strengthened, and we find that we begin to understand more deeply what our faith means, to us and to those with whom we speak.

The principle here is simple: learning through teaching. In order to teach any subject effectively, it is necessary to prepare, to formulate the material to be taught. As we formulate the material, it becomes something that we can claim as our own, not simply information loosely connected to our experience. We must do more than know the information - we must own it.

The Challenge to Ownership

The process of this ownership can be seen in "THE DISC OF LIFE" by Charles M. Tanner. Paul Hornsby is the host of a late-night radio call-in show, "Nostalgia Beat". He is a Christian, but has never truly shared about his faith, until a call comes in, from a person who identifies herself only as "Kim".

Kim wishes to know why Paul is so positive, what the source of his happiness, his "turn-on", his sense of purpose is. Paul, used to having people tell him of their problems, is not at all prepared to talk about himself, and it is only after a great deal of evasiveness that he finally agrees to talk about his faith.

Paul You're blackmailing me.

Kim I can't do that.

Paul Oh, yes you can. You're backing me into a corner.

Kim If you're somehow afraid to hang up, I will.

Paul That's not the point, and you know it. You're using my conscience against me.

Kim I have no control over your conscience.

Paul I wish I did.

Paul senses that, once he has embarked on this path, it may lead him into areas that could be uncomfortable for him. Sharing one's faith in a one-on-one situation is daunting enough as it is, but over the phone in the middle of the night makes it more so. Kim has described Paul as her 'last hope", and driven by the thought of what she may do if he refuses her outright, Paul finally overcomes his embarrassment and self-consciousness:

Paul Let me tell you all I can. I believe in God. I am, in fact, a Christian.

Kim You are? By commitment or by birth?

Paul By birth? Oh, I see what you mean. Someone whose parents attended church and so he does - kind of.

Kim Kind of. Yes.

Paul No. No, that's not the way it is with me. I am - uh committed.

As Paul continues to speak, he begins to understand his own faith more clearly. He finds that his faith does indeed stem from a real relationship with Jesus, and thanks to Kim, Paul realizes just how precious to Him God's love is.

Kim Do you really believe God loves you?

Paul Yes. Yes, I know it. He really does love me. (Pause) And you, too.

Kim About this joy.

Paul It fills you. It's an inexplicable kind of joy. I mean, it's not like getting a new car or something. That's understandable, and quickly passes away. We tend to take such things for granted. But this other joy stays, and since you don't know exactly what it is it's always rare and inexplicable... You really know God loves you, and that there's nothing more exciting in all of life than that.

Kim	Life.

Paul	Yes, life. We seem to have circled back to that, haven't we?

Kim	Yes.

Paul	Well, that's it. God, Christ, Love, Fulfillment, Joy, Agape, Turn-on.

Kim	You feel that - all the time?

Paul	Oh yeah, I mean how could you let it go once you feel that really completeness inside. It's got to be a full time thing. Who would settle for less? Ever.

Having been the catalyst for Paul's realization, Kim quickly hangs up, leaving Paul with the question: what was Kim's purpose in calling? To find a purpose herself, or to awaken Paul to the full depths of his own commitment? To quote Paul himself: "Who saved whom?"

By bringing Paul through this process of thought, "THE DISC OF LIFE" brings us down a similar path. Audience comments from the play reflect the fact that this process has served not only to strengthen the faith of the fictional Paul Hornsby, but countless of audience members as well:

"I saw two major points in that play: there are people out there who are hurting and people who can help them."

"I saw my life up there."

"That play really challenged me - he talked about things that I am dealing with in my life now."

"I used to be a disc-jockey, and I know that people do call in like that. I worked at night on week-ends and I've never had an experience quite like that, but it was still very real to me."

"I was sitting where I could see the congregation and during ("DISC OF LIFE"). I saw many eyes filled with tears and some wet cheeks." (Quesnel, British Columbia)

(From an Army chaplain in Mainz, Germany) "I was afraid that you almost lost them during the disc jockey play, for they were very quiet. Then I realized that it was because they were involved."

(From one of his men) "That play was great. I really needed that. I've only been a Christian for a year, and it's really hard for me to talk about - mostly because I'm afraid to. I'm still afraid, but not as much. That was a really good play to do. A lot of the guys here are searching, but most of them don't know what for. Maybe some of them do now."

"I really enjoyed it tonight. I brought along my Muslim friend. I think she enjoyed it. I was challenged tonight. As I am discovering with my Muslim friend, it is not easy to share your faith at times. Like in your play." (Tours, France)

"I believe it is very clear, that is to say, one can't ignore the message while you listen to this play. One can see what you mean to say and I think that is important. Sometimes we try to avoid God - I know I'm a bit like that - but when something like this happens, it isn't possible, you need to listen. It touched me. Well done." (Gaubert, France)

"What you do certainly makes one think. It is interesting because it shows that Christians must do their homework. The Christian must be someone who can speak of his faith very easily, like you showed us in your play. It is very important." (Malmedy, Belgium)

"I don't really know what to say. I don't want to go on ... that play... well, I'm sure you feel the same (murmurs of consent from the assembly) ... there is so much to think about ... (a tear sparkling in the corner of his eye, wiped away) ... I don't know how - long it has been,

since I have heard ... the Gospel given in such a - personal, moving - way... There was so much, I am still thinking - but thank you." (The main speaker, after the play was performed for a conference in the former East Germany)

"I can't understand it, but we who have day-to-day jobs find it so hard to be open about Jesus. We work beside people who need to hear, just like Kim, but we wait for them to ask before offering. I guess it's good that you don't give us direct answers, even though at the moment I think differently. Because if you did, there would be no need for us to think about it any further, and the answers you would give us wouldn't help - it would be easily forgotten." (Vienna, Austria)

"I wish you could have been here in the audience at the point when Paul admitted he was a Christian. You could have heard a pin drop on a marshmallow." (Munich, Germany)

"It was really a gift - a gift from the Lord. There are no words... That someone could be so changed, through the Lord. That was from life... and Kim - she wasn't a character - she was a mirror for many people here. You were both mirrors - a way for us to change. It wasn't just a story, it really was from daily life." (Munich, Germany)

"That play was so special, so many of the questions that Kim had are questions that I've asked myself. It was very good for me to hear those answers, and how real they were for Paul."

It is significant that both Paul of "THE DISC OF LIFE" and Gina of "CHRISTMAS EVE" first come to a full realization of what has taken place as they are in prayer after all has occurred. We often require that short moment in God's presence in order to gain new insight into ourselves, and to realize that we have indeed grown, have been stretched, through the challenge of experience.

Chapter 6

THE STATE OF INNER HELL

There is another side of the spiritual element, which is based in and thrives on the negative side of the Spirit. This is an area that is often entered by the action of denying the Spirit. I must emphasize here that there is a significant difference between a man who has denied the Holy Spirit and one whose awareness has yet to be awakened to God.

The distinction can be seen, for example, in the difference between the Pharisees and the Ethiopian official of Acts Chapter 8. The Pharisees were well versed in the tenets of their religion, and presumably in the reality of God, and yet they denied the very Messiah for whom those tenets were meant to prepare them. The Ethiopian, on the other hand, had no relationship with the Lord, and, but for the Lord providing him instruction by means of Philip, might well have lived out his life without completely understanding God, but still have lived a real commitment to Him (as one to whom, as Paul says in Romans, "Faith has been accredited as righteousness").

To any individual who honestly seeks God, God will come. But the man who knows God and denies Him must actively reinforce his denial. To reinforce denial of God, one must dwell on those things that will strengthen the separation. As one concentrates upon divorcing himself from his Creator, certain reactions are developed, habitual reactions to touches on the spirit, reactions that slowly develop into a protective cocoon, in which the individual can hide from God (atheists perversely refer to this as "developing an open mind").

For such a person, Hell has already begun, just as Heaven has already opened for those who accept Christ. The "Sabbath rest" of Hebrews and the torments of the damned are both very real experiences of the everyday lives of many mortals.

Tracing the Path Down

Portraying the temporal states of Heaven or Hell is a delicate task, because we humans have tremendous difficulty in separating the condition of an individual from the individual himself. A man who, in ignorance, utters a "chauvinistic" remark may suddenly find himself bearing the total responsibility of the inequality of women. A person who, out of personal reasons, snaps at his co-workers, might soon become identified as the "office grouch". A woman may be labeled as "scatterbrained" on the basis of one non-sequitur. We are very quick to label others, and very slow to understand them.

The same applies, unfortunately, to the view of most Christians toward those who separate themselves from Christ. We are quick to condemn the apostate, and slow to learn what has driven them to seek apostasy. And in our quickness to condemn, we fail to see the true tragedy of the inner state of Hell, i.e., its avoidability.

To trace the path out, we must trace the path in, and that path is very easily entered. We often picture Hell as a place of torture, and ignore the fact that we torture ourselves in a number of ways, often for no or little reason.

The Singlet

An advantage of drama is that it affords us the opportunity to view a character in those moments when no others are present. The most commonly used method to achieve this is the soliloquy. A soliloquy is a reflective moment inserted into the larger context of a play. The term reflects that a character is alone, or at least not aware of others around him. This is in contrast to a monologue, which is addressed to a specific audience. The soliloquy is dependent on the play's context to give it an identity (Shakespeare's "Hamlet" soliloquy is often presented by itself, in the assumption of knowledge of the play's context by its audience).

For the repertoire of Covenant Players, Charles M. Tanner has developed a form of play quite similar to a soliloquy in its outward form, but vastly different in its structure: the Singlet. This term is applied to those plays in which one person appears alone, thus the similarity to the soliloquy. But here the similarity ends. Singlets are fully plays unto themselves, though perforce of a shorter length, generally speaking, with all of the elements of conflict and resolution contained, and conclusions drawn, positively or negatively.

The format of the Singlet provides an optimal framework to trace the path into one's inner hell. The play, "THE DEFEAT" by Charles M. Tanner depicts one such path, taken by Lissa Franklin, a woman who is struggling with alcoholism. Finally unable to deal with her sickness on her own, and seeing no hope or help, Lissa comes to a desperate decision:

> Who can I turn to? Who can help me? God? How many times have I prayed to Him for help? The thousand again? At least. And has He helped me? (Angrily) No! IF He exists, He's sure ignoring me. I even attended church for a while. He didn't seem to notice that, either. No, that's no way for help. There IS no way for help, Lissa - you lush. You might as well face it. (Low and defeated tones) Go and get your bottle and pour it down. You won't even enjoy it anymore. You just do it because you have to have it. So you'll do it. And you'll keep on doing it until finally - everyone will have left you and you'll just curl up and somewhere with the cheapest bottle you can find and - die.

"THE DEFEAT' is a study in despair. It reflects the hopelessness not only of the alcoholic, but of anyone caught in the miasma of a habit or addiction they cannot control. In a sense, the play provides an excellent refutation for those who accuse Christians as a group of a kind of 'pie-in-the-sky" attitude. Lissa does not find her way to salvation on her own, neither in the sense of her alcoholism nor in an eschatological sense. If she is to be rescued, it must come from outside of herself. She has cried out to God, and God must indeed answer.

Agents of Salvation

God's answer comes in another Singlet, "KEEP LOOKING - YOU'LL FIND IT'. In this play the Lord challenges a woman, Melody Newman, to put into action her concern for people who are being ignored. The catalyst for this concern is a newspaper article:

> Here a woman's husband dies and after the funeral and first offers of help everyone begins to drift away, move back, slide out of the picture - and almost immediately she is ignored - shunned even. That is a terrible thing to do...

Most of us have uttered similar phrases, and let our concern stop there. Melody, however, is not content with mere lip service to the problem:

> Something's got to be done about it. We ought to set up a committee in the church to help our own, at least, when they have troubles, problems. (There is a pause) We DO have such a committee in our church. Well, they ought to be more available. They do have a line in the bulletin that anyone in need of counseling should call this number ... Wait a minute. There was Sheila Grant. She had a problem, but she wouldn't call. She told me later she did not want COUNSELLING; she just wanted someone to talk to, to care

Again, we hear phrases that we well may have used ourselves, but Melody's train of thought is not yet finished:

> Wait a minute! Someone - ought. Who? (Makes a face) Yes, yes, dear over-working conscience, I know. You, of course, immediately volunteer me ... I wonder if everyone's conscience is as loud and insistent as mine? All right. Me. Because it has come to me.

Having come to herself, she must now identify where the need lies that she is to minister to, and in that process, one name comes instantly to mind:

> But - I mean Lissa Franklin may NOT WANT any help. I mean, it's her business isn't it? So she drinks. Am I her judge? Am I her - Ooooooops? I had to ask. Her - keeper.

Melody has bridged an important gap - that which lies between the identification of a problem requiring a solution, and the personal conversion of the identification into concrete action. She knows that there is a need. More importantly, she knows precisely where that need exists. She must respond to that need - or sacrifice a substantial portion of her own self-respect.

Defining Tough Love

Melody has gotten the message. She must now act upon it. This brings us to the third play in this trilogy, "THE SOLUTION, NOT THE METHOD".

As Melody arrives at Lissa's door, she is confronted with a shocking difference between her expectations of committed service for the Lord and the reactions that that service brings forward. Far from accepting Melody as a bold witness for God, Lissa unleashes a wave of bitterness against her, and all that she represents in Lissa's mind:

Lissa (Snaps angrily and makes an ugly face) I don't need any help. I don't need His and I don't need yours. Gimme my glass and the door's over that way.

Melody (Sighs, hands the glass over) You DO need help. And you know it.

Lissa And don't send anyone else to come visiting. I don't want you. I won't listen. You and anyone like you'll just be wasting your time. Yours and mine. (Shouts it) Go on, get out!

Melody (A pained look, she's failed, sighs and turns) I'm sorry.

Lissa Sure you are. So am I. You'd like to be a heroine. And I'd like to be -

Melody (Turns at the door) I COULD help. Honestly.

Lissa Keep goin'. You have nothing to say to me. (Melody sighs and leaves - Lissa speaks in a lower voice) I tried God and He wouldn't help me.

By this time we have reached far past the accepted limits of normal missioning activity. Very few people would blame Melody for leaving in the face of such determined negativity. It is therefore surprising to see her return, and all the more so to discover what has driven her to do so:

Melody (With energy but not emotion at this point) Did you say you tried God and He wouldn't help?

Lissa (Glares anew) I though you'd gone. Keep goin'. (Melody doesn't move and clearly shows she has no intention to move, in fact advances a few steps back into the room) Yeah, yeah. (Said to hurt Melody) That's what I said. I tried 'im. He wouldn't - or couldn't - help. (Hard) Nothin'.

Melody (Somewhat hard back) Why on earth did you suppose He would?

Lissa (Taken aback) Whaddya mean? He's supposed to help people.

Melody (Still hard, moving further into the room) On whose terms? Yours? What were they, by the way? Or did you bother including yourself into the bargain at all?

Lissa I don't know what you're talkin' - talking about.

Melody (Almost angry) Everyone expects God to answer their prayers exactly the way they want them to be answered. Or else! Or else what, Lissa? You'll drink yourself to death, just to show Him?

Lissa You're getting insulting.

Melody (Hard) I can't insult you. Look at you! Bottle in one hand, full glass of booze in the other, swaying about. You've spilled all over the carpet and yourself. Not to mention me in the bargain.

Lissa (Hisses it loudly) Get out!

Melody (Hard and angry) No. I like you. I am your friend. What's more, I insist on being your sister. At least this morning. If you never see me again, I must know that I got involved – once at least - to try to save your life.

Lissa (Nearly a scream) I don't want you to save my life! (Tears come) Can't you see, I'm trying to hurry it up so I can have some peace. (A cry, deep and extended) I want to die!

The closer one comes to a wound, the more intense the pain caused. The more intense the pain, the stronger the reaction to it. If we truly intend to be our brother's keeper, we must be prepared to withstand the fires of our brother's hell. The agents of the Lord are no weak-willed innocents, as so often characterized by those who do not wish to join them. They are people of intense faith, and a strength made especially supple by the guidance of the Holy Spirit.

In depicting the Hell-inside, we must always remember that our purpose is hope. We, as Christians, know in whom our hope is based, and we know that the Living God who gives us that hope is universal. Since God is universal, hope is also universal. Therefore, we do not depict the Hell-inside for its own sake, to be titillated by visions of mental or emotional horror. We project the view of life without God to illuminate the eternal hope of Jesus the Savior.

Chapter 7

THE GROWTH OF RELATIONSHIP

Any individual who involves himself with drama over an extended period of time finds himself, sooner or later, personally involved in the lives and developments of the people portrayed (it is for this reason that TV soap operas continue to command such large followings). This applies just as strongly to those who are actively involved in the preparation and performance of a play, as to those who view the presentation. For those who are active in drama on a full-time basis, this involvement can become a deep relationship, in which a part of oneself is directly invested in the character.

In the unique environment of Covenant Players, one in which the performers and the playwright are not only involved as business partners, but also in a teacher/pupil situation, this in-depth relationship is put to use as an opportunity to increase the capacities of both. The result is a genre of plays referred to as the "Life Series". Covering a myriad of topics and time-spans, these plays have evolved out of the need, on the part of the audience, to know more about the characters that they have come to know.

Lessons of History

The projection of imagination is essential in dealing with history. The historian does not simply report the events of the past. He attempts also to analyze those events and decisions, to draw parallels to the present and to the future, to draw conclusions based upon the available facts and what can be deduced from the human nature and characters of the people specifically involved.

Often, the conclusions drawn by the historian contain too much detail for the majority of people to understand and benefit from them. Instead, the number of facts and figures only serve to confuse them further. At other times, the tangible evidence available is too little to justify the leap of intuition needed to complete the picture. In both cases, it becomes the communicator's task to interpret the results into a more universal form.

Communicative drama provides an illustration of such conclusions, available for a more general audience. A major element of these illustrations is the view of the predominant attitudes of the time portrayed. We cannot assume that our values have been shared by every culture and time of history. Different ages place value on different things. On the other hand, we may also not assume that our present attitudes are unique to our age, for they are borne of our incorrigible humanness. By seeing the attitudes that led to an historic event, we can see how closely our own age parallels them, and some possible outcomes that may be embraced or avoided.

The Personalities of History

We tend to think of history in terms of certain prominent individuals. Certain names stand out as having affected their particular eras, or as indicative of the character of a given period, such as the Victorian or Alexandrian periods, etc. But there is a value to a view of history's personalities beyond mere identification. For the most part, we know the consequences of the decisions made by various personages of the past, and it is therefore enlightening to view the basic stages of formation that led them to those decisions.

Charles M. Tanner has provided the Covenant Players repertoire with various historical series. Some examples are:

GEORGE ARMSTRONG CUSTER: The rise to power and prominence of a military leader who is known chiefly for the worst decision he made.

QUEEN VICTORIA: The early years of a queen who gave not only a name, but an atmosphere, to an entire era. This series began with her ascension to the throne, and brings not only Victoria into focus, but also her first Prime Minister, Lord Melbourne (the unique character of yet another of Victoria's PMs, Benjamin Disraeli, is illuminated in another series).

GAVRILLO PRINZIP: An in-depth analysis of the series of stupidities and overreactions that led to the First World War, within the context of the man who touched them off, the assassin of Austria's Crown Prince.

MATA HARI: The roots of the famous dancer's demise, and her final entrapment in events beyond her control, analyzed through her attitude towards her own life.

ELIZABETH I: The resilience of a regnant queen in an era hostile to her assuming such a role.

ABRAHAM LINCOLN: The early internal struggles, too often left unmentioned, of the Lincoln Administration.

Such plays give us the unique opportunity to meet the individuals who have contributed so greatly to Man's heritage. We are allowed to view them in their own environment, to experience their individual values, pressures and ambitions along with them. And as we do so, we begin to understand that these were real, living human beings, much like ourselves.

Are the depictions accurate? Not in terms of recorded chronological history, no. But in terms of the character's essence, and the communicative power of historical experience - the ability to communicate through the ages to us in our own situations - indeed they are.

Capturing the Essence of History

One example may serve to illustrate the accuracy of these historical depictions. A Singlet, entitled "WHOEVER YOU ARE", was written by Charles M. Tanner, to depict Dietrich Bonhoeffer on the eve of his execution in the Flossenburg Concentration Camp in 1945. In 1987 a unit of Covenant Players performed the play for a group of British chaplains in Luebbeke, Germany. The leader of that unit, Ron Cook, reported afterwards that, following the performance, the unit was approached by Professor Eberhard Bethge, a close relative of Dietrich Bonhoeffer, who had been deeply moved by the play. According to the report, Professor Bethge told the unit, 'That's it! The play really captured exactly how Dietrich thought about death... it was the other death. The difference between death in general and death that meets you on the inside."

Later that day, lecturing to the chaplains, Professor Bethge referred back to the play: *"On April 9, 1945 ... (here he stopped with a catch in his throat and looked at the performers, sitting in the front row) ... Thank you again for doing that (play) this morning. I was very moved. It was almost - too much for me."*

He spoke once more with the unit as they were leaving the conference: *'Thank you again for your special work. Dealing with the last moments of a man is so delicate. For his family and friends, to think about those days is very difficult. This play was almost too much. But I can say, from what I understand, that what you did - for me, it was possible. Yes. You have such a privilege to be able to share this man with people. To communicate who he really was. I want you to continue - it touched me."*

Anonymous Contributions to History

History does not revolve solely on the names that have survived to our time, however. The impact of unknown individuals upon history is just as strong. Accordingly, Charles Tanner's writing also includes various series concerning those who have been caught up in history's events.

Many such plays highlight people or groups that have been largely ignored by subsequent generations, such as 'The USS Torquay", which recounts the contribution of the Submarine Corps, the so-called "silent service" of the United States Navy, to the winning of the War in the Pacific.

Two other areas of contribution from the same period are documented in 'The Ferry Queens" and 'The Eaglettes", two series which deal with, respectively, the British and the American women pilots who ferried planes in support of their male counterparts in active service on the front.

It is indeed a privilege to have these plays, not only to be able to involve oneself with the known and unknown heroes of history, but also to afford others the opportunity to know them more intimately. Whatever form the historical Life Series may take, the effect is to raise our view, to partake in a portion of the greatness of the past, and, hopefully, to acquire a taste of that greatness, that we may then carry into our own lives.

Unique Christian Individuals

Historical plays deal, for the most part, with unique events and periods of time. But not all of Charles Tanner's Life Series are historical. Many deal with everyday people who are unique in themselves. These are people who could be encountered anywhere, but cannot help but leave their mark on all with whom they come in contact.

I'd like to cite three characters as examples. The first is Maurice, a character who was first encountered in the periphery of a play entitled, "THE SOLID SIEVE". This background character, at first glance a simple bartender, aroused such interest in the play's first audience, that a play was written to provide the opportunity to identify more of him. There is considerably much more to identify. In subsequent plays, Maurice has proven to be a man of surprising wit and resourcefulness. He is a bartender on purpose, having accepted as his service to Christ the ministry to those who come to his bar. In providing an open ear, coupled with a wealth of knowledge and sensitivity, to those who could otherwise remain unreached by conventional evangelism, Maurice is an excellent pattern of Christian witness in today's world.

Similar in task, though divergent in character, Lance Cpl. Alfred White, more popularly known as 'The Badger". Badger is a simple soldier in the trenches of World War I, and also a Christian of unusual depth. The power of Badger's witness lies in his simplicity. Being a Cockney with little formal education, Badger has had very little training in the convolutions of theological thinking. He has read and reads the Bible, however, and has an unique capacity to listen to the Lord's leading ("nudges", as he terms them).

Armed with these alone, Badger has confounded many "sophisticated" minds, confronting them with the reality of a direct, personal relationship with Jesus Christ, in every setting and background of his war-torn environment.

Sabella Horton, our third example, occupies the rarified world of Park Avenue, New York. She is an accomplished editor of children's books, and a woman of tremendous energy and intelligence. She is also, no less than Badger or Maurice, unquestionably aware of the personal reality of Jesus the Christ. Both she and Badger witness in much the same way: in the words of Badger, they 'just talk". Badger simply speaks what is on his mind. Sabella uses her words as an artist, weaving them into a tapestry, upon which the truths she is communicating can be mounted and illuminated. She herself explains her purpose in "SABELLA AND THE KILLER": "The solution to the communication is to listen to the synthesis of what I say and let the words fall and flow around you as per my design."

One major binding tie between the character of Maurice, Badger and Sabella is that of humility. In the very action of powerful witness for Christ, all three have, at different times, expressed the wish that they could do more. Sabella is driven to make each human contact into an opportunity to minister, by the very fact that she has been found medically unfit for overseas mission work. Maurice has placed himself purposely in the position of bartender, as a means of ministering to those who seek solace in drink. Badger intends to study further when the war is over, but in the meantime seeks to be used as the Lord would use him - and the Lord does so unceasingly.

In these three series, as well as others dealing with the many common/uncommon servants of God, we find what may be as close to a common theme as we may apply to Charles Tanner's works: that Christianity cannot, will not be limited to exclude any location, situation, time, race, physical or social structure. Wherever God's people may find themselves, be it the agricultural Midwest, the boxing world, the world of a jazz percussionist, a blind painter or a long-inactive actress returning to Hollywood, or the treacherous peril of the French Resistance - even amidst the horrors of a German concentration camp - God is there, wherever His human beings are, and He call us, those who bind our beings to His name, to be His wherever we may find ourselves.

Chapter 8

BIBLICAL PLAYS - ENACTING THE GOSPEL

Drama as a medium is dichotomous. It is at once concrete and impulsive. It confronts us simultaneously with the visual, the tangible, that which can be grasped, and the intangible, the amorphic, that which can only be felt. To do so, it plays upon our own universal identification points, those points at which we may personally identify with what we view.

It is for this reason that the portrayal of Biblical scenes presents us with unique challenges - especially those of the Gospels. When dealing with the characters of history, the social or political strata of the present, the various interpretations of celestial or infernal beings, even the anthropomorphic personifications of animals or inanimate objects, we are still dealing with creations; things which are finite, which have had an origin, may be placed somewhere within our parameters of reference, and still remain distinct and apart from us.

God, on the other hand, is no creation, but Creator. It is He who placed us within our parameters in the first place, and who, through the power of His redemption, raises us beyond them. He is infinitely beyond our powers of conception, both concrete and amorphic, and yet, infinitely more intimate as well.

Jesus was an individual, unique human being, and, at the same time, the eternal God. In His humanness He was like no other human being that ever existed. It is for this reason that Charles Tanner has stated that he will never write a play that directly depicts Jesus. Despite Mr. Tanner's vast experience and talent as a playwright, he could do no more than scratch the surface of the true nature of the Christ. Nor could he expect even the finest actor to give an adequate portrayal of the part, no matter how inspired the performance. Certain of his plays may contain "Christ figures", but these are strictly designed to present an allegory of certain aspects of Christ, within the context of the play in which they appear.

Beards and Bathrobes

By Charles Tanner's own account, it was some time before he wrote any plays at all dealing with individuals in the Bible. His reservations stemmed, by his own admittance, from his personal experiences with the standard of amateur dramatics in the Church at that time - a style Mr. Tanner refers to as "Beard and Bathrobe" drama. His aim in founding the Covenant Players was to utilize modem-day drama, to put the principles of Christian living in the context of our present experience. He sought to bring Christianity into the now.

Mr. Tanner's breakthrough came when he was requested to write a play dealing with the Apostle Paul. After much hesitation, he wrote a three-act play entitled "THE HIGH CALLING". The response to that play was tremendous, and led Mr. Tanner to an important discovery - that the conditions of Bible times contain the same potential for dramatic conflict and action as the present day. The Bible depicts people as they interact with one another - essentially, drama itself.

This discovery led to an entirely new venue of dramatic expression for Charles Tanner. These plays go beyond the simple conversion of the written words of the Bible into visible form. Through these "Biblical" plays, we are given an insight into the life and times of those people who, for most of us, have heretofore been merely literary figures, two-dimensional characters lacking the depth necessary for us to truly take their experiences to heart.

Through Charles Tanner's Biblical plays, we are given the chance to meet the followers of God in their own element, with all of their foibles, weakness and stumbling blocks, as they learn through their own mistakes the lessons of God that they have passed on to us through the Scriptures.

Here we may meet a Paul who, burning as he may be with the fire and conviction of the Holy Spirit, also faces frustration and struggle, to communicate his deep understanding of the sacrifice and resurrection of Jesus to those around him. Here we may meet a Peter who, filled as he is with the strength and drive to fulfill the Lord's commission given to him, also may return to the agonizing moment when he committed the heinous crime of willfully denying his allegiance to Jesus, at the moment his Lord needed him most.

Here we may also meet Judas, a man compelled by his fervent wish to see Jesus acclaimed a conquering Messiah according to his own concept of the role, and haunted to his own suicide by the sickening betrayal that wish has led him to make. Or Pontius Pilate, a man torn between a deep sense of personal integrity and the seemingly imperative requirements of political expediency, faced at every cusp with blind alleys, and frustrated at every turn by wrong choices.

Here we also meet the women, so often overlooked in the greater movement of the Bible's events. Claudia Procula, the wife of Pilate, a woman of patrician birth seeking to reconcile the deep impact Jesus has had on her mind and heart with her commitment to support her husband in his advancement through the political arenas of Rome. Martha, who, along with her sister Mary, must learn to reprioritize the accepted practicalities of their lives. Lydia, a woman of keen mind and fervent conviction for the Lord, who must deal with her deep frustration at the limitations placed upon her by the culture in which she has been born and now lives.

Here we may also meet the nameless, the obscure figures, who come and go briefly in the Scriptures' accounts. Such an individual forms the focus of Charles Tanner's play, "THE ALABASTER JAR". One of Mr. Tanner's more recent plays, it takes place outside of a house in Bethany, where a prominent man is speaking. The house is being guarded by Jacob, a young man who has incurred some gambling debts and now must work them off. A woman, Mary (the name Mary was common in many forms in Judaea at the time - this is not one of the Marys with which we are familiar) arrives, and begins to enter the house, only to be stopped by Jacob.

As Jacob begins to inquire after the young woman's business, he notices that she is carrying a jar made of alabaster, which contains a very fragrant substance:

Jacob Is that perfume in there? (Startled) It can't be. The jar is too big. If that were filled with - perfume - it would be worth a fortune. (Beat) ... and the likes of you would never be able to afford something like that.

Mary (Calmly) It is perfume. But a perfume oil. (Sighs and hopeful) Which is more valuable than the essence alone. (Hugs the jar momentarily) It must be very valuable. As worthy as anything that would be available - (looks off mistily and speaks mystically) for it must be as 'sacred' to man as it hopefully will be to God.

Jacob is a Sadduccee, and as such is not very impressed by the discussion inside. He is, however, very impressed by the jar, and its potential value if he can get it out of Mary's hands.

Mary	Dear friend, have you stood here at the door and not listened to He who speaks and teaches the secrets of LIFE? (She gestures inside the room)

Jacob	(Stares at her) You mean - Him. The strange one. The Galilean?

Mary	(Smiles) He is a great man - a great prophet - a man so close to God, no one has ever heard such teaching before.

Jacob	(Stares into the room) Hey, I'm paid to watch the door. It gets too crowded and someone gets sick - always happens. The owner doesn't want any sick around this - (gestures) HIM.

Mary	(Laughs) That is funny. This man, this prophet, heals people who are sick. It would not bother Him.

When Jacob makes it clear that Mary cannot enter the house, Mary resolves to wait until the meeting is over and those inside come out. Jacob, remembering the alabaster jar, offers to buy it from Mary, or to sell it for a share of the profits.

Mary	It is not for sale. Not for any price. (Gently, wishing him to understand but knowing he cannot) I have been commanded to do - what I must do with this ointment.

Jacob	(Starts to get sarcastic again, but stops it fast) You've been commanded! (The change, the smile) Look, think about it. What you could do with –

Mary (Nods) I have. I will. (Looks inside, shrugs) It should happen now - I don't know why but I feel it strongly. (Nods) But I will wait if that is what is necessary.

Finally, Jacob offers to let Mary enter - if she will bring the jar back out with her. Mary agrees, with one stipulation of her own.

Jacob I'll let you in but it will be your responsibility in case it gets too tough - AND you WILL bring the alabaster jar back out – and WILL NOT run away without talking to me.

Mary (A wicked gleam in her eye) But you must promise something, too. (Smiles) When I return - if I am not stopped inside and I get to do what I have been commanded - I will GIVE you the jar - if you give me your word you will talk to the man who is now teaching in that room.

Jacob (Thinks - what's the catch - the trick - how could there be in that, chuckles) Sure. Of course, I'll talk to him. To anybody. But how do I know which one it is? (Sniffs) They're all talking - they're Jews aren't they. (Laughs) And it IS all about religion - of course. (Pause) Which one?

Mary (Gently) The Rabbi - the one His disciples call the Master. (Lovingly) Jesus of Nazareth.

Mary is, of course, the same woman who anointed Jesus' feet, as recounted in the three synoptic Gospels. The house is that of Simon, and although Mary will keep her promise to bring the jar back out with her, it will have in the meantime been emptied - in a powerfully symbolic act which will be remembered throughout history.

In this play we see practically illustrated the principle which makes Charles Tanner's biblical plays such an invaluable resource for the church today. These plays convey a sense of vividness to the Scriptures. We see the "real lives" of the Bible, and in the light of those "real lives", it becomes clear to us that we, in our "real lives", are no less involved in the Lord's reality and His actions among us. Through these Bible-based plays, we begin to truly understand that the Lord Jesus is indeed "the same yesterday, today and tomorrow ".

Chapter 9

WATCHING THE HOLY SPIRIT AT WORK

When Jesus returned to His Father, He sent, according to His promise to His disciples, the Comforter; God's own Spirit, a constant guide and companion, and, in a sense, God's personal 'stake' in us. It is curious that this Holy Spirit, that element of the Truine God that should be the most concrete and intimately knowable, is so difficult to grasp for so many Christians.

No direct portrayal of the Holy Spirit is adequate to convey everything that He is or can be for each of us individually. The changes that the Spirit of God causes to take place in the heart can only be seen in the actions those changes bring about. And it is here that communicative drama can be used to excellent effect.

Insight

There are moments when the whole of our understanding seems to equal more then the sum of its parts. Suddenly, for no particular reason, a word or phrase will open an entirely unexpected venue of insight into the understandings and viewpoints of those with whom we are speaking, or the situation in which we find ourselves. These sudden flashes of insight are often based upon information which we have already received, and long relegated to the further reaches of our memory. Only the touch and timing of the Holy Spirit is capable of recalling them into a newer, deeper structure of understanding.

We find evidence of such works of the Spirit in Genesis, as Joseph interprets first the dreams of two servants of Pharaoh, and then those of Pharaoh himself. In the book of Daniel, the young prophet not only is empowered by the Lord to interpret the dream of King Nebucadnezzar, but he is even able to tell the king precisely what it is that he dreamt.

We have already discussed the character of The Badger. What this character identifies as the Lord's "nudges" are none other than this same movement of the Spirit. Such "nudges" come to anyone, depending on the needs of those involved, as defined by the Lord in His wisdom. This even applies when the individual involved is the Christian himself. In numerous Singlets involving the Badger himself, we see him impacted by the Spirit's sudden insight into his own words.

The Charles Tanner play, "AND THE WALLS CAME TUMBLING DOWN" provides us with a view of the tangible application of this principle. The play takes place in Konstanz, Germany, at a border crossing between Germany and Switzerland. A young Christian woman, Mary, is seeking entry into Germany in order to have an operation done by a specialist in Munich. As so often is the case, she is turned down, by a border official who appears to have no concern for her whatsoever:

Mary (Sighs) As I told you, I am going to Munich for a special operation. (Sighs again) I'm afraid I must have it.

Heinrich (This he understands) But there are fine doctors in Switzerland.

Mary (Warmly) Indeed there are. Else my diagnosis would not have turned up the reason I need to go to Munich.

Heinrich (Shrugs) Have the operation in Suisse.

Mary (Shakes her head) The only doctor who can handle my case is in Munich. (Looks off) It is very rare. The Munich man is a specialist. (Pause) The only other such is in Baltimore.

Heinrich (Firmly) You must go there then. Your passport is not in order.

Mary (Startled) Do you know how far Baltimore is from here? How much it would cost to get there?

Heinrich Baltimore will be much better.

Mary (A near cry) I cannot go to Baltimore. I cannot afford it. The operation will be very expensive.

Heinrich (Shrugs) That is not my problem. (Nods, tight-faced) Your passport is not in order.

It should be noted that Heinrich is not intended to be a stereotyped German. In fact, border officials all over the world tend to exhibit the same attitudes.

Having received neither hearing nor encouragement from this official encounter, Mary is tempted to be despondent. She is brought out of this temptation when she encounters another woman, Teresa, who has been denied entry to the country due to a broken exhaust pipe on her car, which, it being a holiday, cannot be repaired, at least not to the satisfaction of the authorities. Despite the mitigating circumstances, and the fact that she and her husband must be in Hamburg the following day to catch a ship, the two have been required to obtain official certification before they can enter Germany.

As the two women talk, their conversation turns to the guards with whom they have been talking. Suddenly, Mary experiences a flash of insight:

Mary The man I've been dealing with is all tight-faced. Worried, you know. (Double takes) Worried? (Stares and evaluates) My goodness. Worried? Why of course he is. He is most anxious and deeply disturbed. (Quickly comes alive) Excuse me. I must see if I can help that man. (And she hurries over to the counter)

Heinrich (Looks up - doesn't even sigh) Bitte?

Mary (Stands, looks a moment, then) You're in trouble.

Heinrich (His eyes widen, he looks around) What? Why do you say that? What is happening? (Looks around almost wildly)

Mary (Shakes her head) No, no, there's no terrorist attack, anything like that. (Nods to him, smiles) I mean you. You have problems. At least a problem. (A gentle smile) It's bothering you very much.

Boldness

Insight has brought Mary to the point of recognizing another's need, but it is here that we see another province of the Holy Spirit: Boldness. The very fact that she has approached Heinrich is, for the young border guard, inconceivable, and serves him such a shock that, before he himself has realized it, he finds himself relating to her what has him so worried:

Heinrich (Looks down and sighs hard) My sister. Young. She has run away from home.

Mary (Quickly) That's terrible. (Pause) When did it happen?

Heinrich (Deep breath) 10 days ago. We cannot find her. No relatives. No friend. Police do not know. No one knows.

Mary (Gently) Have you checked any schools she might have attended? Might be friends you didn't know she had.

Heinrich (Nods) We checked - as best we could. Everything.

Mary (Very gently) Hospitals?

Heinrich (Nods) Every one. (Shrugs) She is gone. (Pause) My parents are older. They are hurt.

Mary (Nods) I imagine so. But they shouldn't leap to conclusions. She probably didn't mean to hurt them.

Heinrich (Shakes his head) No, no, not that way. My parents are hurt because they got very angry with Hilde. Now they feel they drove her away.

It seems that Heinrich's sister is a Christian, and it is this that has irritated his parents so. Mary tells Heinrich that she herself is a Christian, and promises, much to Heinrich's surprise, to pray for him and his family.

As she does so, she is approached by another man, Helmut Prenzel, who has overheard the conversation, and is himself a Christian - a "Follower Christian" (a term that Mary has used with

Heinrich to differentiate from what she calls "Holiday Christians", who only attend church Easter and Christmas). Helmut is also a city official in Konstanz, on his way into Switzerland for his holiday. Mary is at once shocked and ecstatic to hear that Herr Prenzel is an official in - the vehicle division.

In a flurry of activity, Helmut is brought up to date concerning the situation of Teresa, the traveler to Hamburg. Under heavy protest that this is his holiday, and that nothing can be done without returning to his office for the official stamp, he agrees to at least look to see if the broken exhaust has been adequately patched.

As they are gone, Heinrich receives a phone call, but before Mary can talk to him again, the two return. The repair is sufficient, but one problem remains:

Helmut But it needs an official stamp. The stamp is in the office and I am on Holiday.

For Mary, it is once again time for the Holy Spirit's unique combination of insight and boldness:

Mary (Looks up and off a bit) Holiday. (Thinks) Interesting, isn't it? What we humans do to words. Change the pronunciation just a little bit and it changes the meaning almost in reverse. (Smiles anew) Holiday - a time when you serve yourself. Having fun - a good time. Holy Day. How different. A time when you serve the Lord and His needs. Which are always for you NOT to think of yourself.

The significance of Mary's words is not lost on Helmut. With a combination of resignation and the unmistakable traces of real joy, he ushers Teresa off to his office, for a slight delay in his holiday, and a real application of his Holy-Day.

Aura

A third property of the Holy Spirit's presence is its ripple effect. The miracles of the Lord seldom if ever occur in a vacuum. The Spirit touches, and that touch washes over a wide area. Mary has thus far been the catalyst to Teresa's physical aid, and to Helmut's spiritual growth. Now she returns to Heinrich, with a sense of expectancy in her eyes.

Heinrich almost reluctantly relates the news he has received about his sister:

Heinrich She is in a place called Tanzania. (A pause) As missionary. (Pauses again as he stamps viciously) Where she had planned to go all along. The cable from her got lost. (Pause) She is all right.

Mary (Nods) And your parents feel - happier.

Heinrich (Nods, still looking down. Then he picks up some papers and holds them out without looking) These are yours. You may go. (Pause) I made an error in evaluations.

In the wake of this, possibly the greatest miracle in such a situation, Mary does not see the ultimate extent of the aura of her faith. After she leaves - promising to return to talk with Heinrich "about - any questions you may have" - Heinrich finally does look up to where she has been:

Heinrich So I am a holiday Christian. (Long pause, nods) All right. This is a holiday. I shall go to church. (Starts off and mumbles so only the audience can hear) See what happens.

"AND THE WALLS CAME TUMBLING DOWN" gives us a very concrete and practical example of the Holy Spirit's potential for each of us who trust in and receive Him. The reactions of those who have experienced the play attest to the clarity of its lessons:

'That play says quite a bit about how we should act as Christians. I think the person most effected by Mary was the guard. It was great the way it all turned out."

'We may not be seeing any border guards this week ... but there's a whole world out there that needs to hear about Jesus. Go and share the word." (Pastor to his congregation following a performance)

"In the office of the church the next morning, it was fun to hear the pastor telling another man who wasn't at the dinner theater about 'Holiday Christians' and 'Follower Christians'."

"You were really great! A good laugh is good for the soul. It was good. And we laughed, but the message still came through, but not heavy, you know. There were a number of non-Christians there - parents of chidren in our clubs. They don't come very often – they are Holiday Christians, that is the perfect description for them."

'That was really good! I especially liked the one about the border crossing. It really showed what we should be like in any circumstance - really turned on for the Lord and not so tuned in to ourselves."

Insight, Boldness and Aura - three properties which, in the hands of and applied by the Holy Spirit, become very delicate surgical tools, cutting precisely in the needed spots, treating without wounding. Without the Lord's participation, Insight can become viciousness, Boldness arrogance and Aura manipulation. For this reason we are cautioned throughout the New Testament to seek and remain in the Lord, that our dependence on the Holy Spirit may be put to optimum effect.

Chapter 10

MAN IN HIS REASONABLE SACRIFICE - THE PATHWAY PLAYS

The Church of the Middle Ages made use of morality plays to illustrate the types and forms of temptations that Man may encounter in the course of his life, and to provide exhortation to overcome those temptations.

Many examples of this form of literature have found their way down to us, but perhaps the most well-known and dearest of them all can be found in John Bunyan's book, "The Pilgrim's Progress". This allegory is timeless in its parallels of human thought and attitude, and its view of the proper focus in the service of God.

Many versions and adaptations of this work exist, but in the recent decade, Charles M. Tanner has added to the repertoire of Covenant Players a series which, in its clarity and inspiritive power, fully equals and in fact complements Bunyan's classic. This series of plays is known as "The Pathway Series".

This series deals with an individual who is traveling a long path, and though the basic pattern of the plays remains virtually the same, each play is unique in the character of its particular challenge.

The Path Begins

In the very first play of the Pathway Series, "ANYBODY KNOW THE WAY?", the author makes very clear the allegorical nature of the series. This play is set in a wilderness clearing, at the crossing of a number of different roads. A man, Grant, is seated on a bench, as another person, Lee, happens along, evidently trying to decide which pathway to follow (note that names will continue to play a significant role in the course of this series).

Grant, though very much aware of Lee, remains largely uninvolved in her decision. He waits for Lee to initiate their conversation, and does not proffer advice. It is clear from his whole manner that he intends by no means and in no manner to effect the decision which Lee is to make. His most informative words are to identify where she will be able to find the directions that she is seeking:

Lee: I want some directions.

Grant: He gave you those already.

Lee: What do you mean?

Grant: You've got a Bible, haven't you?

Lee: A Bible? (Looks) Of course I've got a Bible.

Grant: There you are.

Lee: How can the Bible act as a travel map for me? It's 2000 years old, for pity's sake.

Grant: Food's even older. You eat, don't you?

Grant offers no further advice, but does respond to Lee's questions, as long as they are placed with purpose, not simply rhetorically:

Lee: Do I have the courage?

Grant: (Points) What does that say?

Lee: About - my courage?

Grant: Uh huh.

Lee: I don't know. I desperately need to know. Won't you tell me that? That one thing?

Grant: You will never be challenged beyond your capacity.

Lee: It - says that?

Grant: Uh huh.

It is significant that Grant does nothing that will effect Lee's decision. Grant identifies himself as "a pretty good guide", but a guide is not an initiator. Grant cannot guide until Lee has committed herself. Any further information can only be had after Lee decides her course.

One begins to recognize the basic pattern of the morality play, but with some vital differences in nuance. Lee has a choice of paths, each one indicated by a different sign. There is a sign made of gold, another draped in royal robes, yet another constructed of stainless steel, and a fourth covered with sugar-coating, accompanied by, in Lee's terms, "handsome guys ... to help you along, another sign said". But Lee is ultimately drawn to a path quite unlike any of the others, a seemingly impassable cliff face, from which a single hand is outstretched.

There is a right path to take, and Lee identifies that it is the cliffface. But it is significant that it is Lee who has made this identification. The decision is not forced upon her. True, Grant indicates that he is this cliffface is the only path that we will help her undertake, but he does not, and in fact cannot, force her to decide to take that path.

Here is an excellent exegesis of the working of the Holy Spirit in us. The Lord does make His paths clear to those who honestly seek them, but He is insistent on leaving the final decision to us.

Since the writing of "ANYBODY KNOW THE WAY" in 1979, audiences all over the world have responded to the depth of its symbolisms. The play has been received particularly well among those who are committed to serving the Lord, either through a mission organization, or simply by taking up a task in their home church. "ANYBODY KNOW THE WAY" allows them to view again the reasons why they made their particular commitments, thereby renewing them.

Stages of the Path

In subsequent plays, Lee will separate herself from her guide, whom she knows by the name of Harry Smith, and experience two essential steps for anyone seeking Christian maturity: the difficulties one encounters by trying to live a Christian life on one's own power, and restoration to full and direct fellowship with the Lord. In the course of this process, Lee receives a new name – Pim – and an essential tool for the remaining journey: a backpack, "for weight, and balance", as its giver tells her.

Pim's path takes her through various stages of growth. In the first stage, she encounters a number of further guides. Some of them seem concerned with aiding her along the path, and towards her final destination. Others appear intent upon distracting her, to make her either leave the path completely, delay her progress, or forsake both her pack, and the Guide Book she is learning to depend upon. As each guide is encountered, Pim's discernment grows, along with her understanding of the price and the nature of the commitment she has made.

After this first stage, the nature of Pim's encounters begins to change. Gradually, she begins to meet fewer guides, and more fellow sojourners, the majority of whom have quite a different view of the path that they are on. Now the temptations are not in terms of individuals who wish to guide her by obvious means, remaining off the path as they do so, but from people who are on the very path that she herself is on, but who seem to have gotten there without the struggle that Pim has gone through.

In a sense, it is a reflection of Pim's spiritual maturity that she can no longer be distracted by the false guides. She has learned to listen and analyze their words in the light of the Guide Book. She has also learned the power of not only resisting the false guides, but in inviting them to join her.

Now, however, Pim begins to come across people who appear to have done so - and have had an easier time of it. At first, this would seem an unfair situation; it seems that Pim has undergone difficulty and hardship to attain a goal that others have reached without nearly so much trouble.

The word "easy", however, touches off an alarm in Pim's mind. Upon investigating further, she discovers an interesting fact: these other travelers have bypassed some of the most difficult stretches of the journey, rendering them both unfit and unwilling to tackle the further challenges that will lead to "The Bridge" - the final destination. Many paths, as Pim discovers, intersect her own. No others lead in the right direction.

Subtle Temptations

A very subtle point in these new temptations is that, often, no effort is made to tell Pim to leave the path. For example, three individuals encountered in the play "STRAIGHT AND NARROW PLUS" have managed to make themselves a cozy home in a clearing not far from the path, which they followed until they "got tired".

The three, Jerry, Beth and Nanny, assure Pim that they fully intend to continue along the path - "someday". They urge Pim to join them, not in order to leave the path, but simply to rest for a time. When Pim resists, they begin to assert a subtle feeling of obligation:

Jerry — Pim, I wonder about you. You sound a little - well - off the boat dock, if you know what I mean.

Beth — (Just a trifle cool) Pim, what we're offering you is very generous and unusual. (Firmly) You must understand that not just everybody gets such an offer.

Nanny — (A bit cool, too) You should not be ungracious, Pim. That would make us think we'd made a mistake in your case.

Jerry — (Makes a face) It is not a very friendly attitude to take. To argue with us and question us and even - (sighs) - deride us for our firm and sure beliefs.

Pim — (Is embarrassed) Oh, I wouldn't think of deriding you for your beliefs. I mean that would be unfair and unjust of me. (A cry) And I do appreciate your kindness and the wonderful offer.

Beth — (A patient, wan smile) Well, that sounds a little better anyway.

Despite her misgivings, and the nagging feeling that something doesn't quite fit, Pim allows herself to be swayed:

Pim — (Struggles, all smile at her, she hates to hurt their feelings) Well, perhaps for a little while.

Jerry — (Waves it off) Don't be silly. Stay a few days and you won't want to move at all. (Look around) This settled down, being in one place, having your own bed and the privacy that goes with it - solid comfort - some luxuries - and Bingo!, that's it. (Nods confidentially) You'll stay.

Beth — And once in a while you can come along here, take a look at that horrible old path and be glad you decided to remain here. Truly.

Nanny — (Laughs quickly) Unless you do like the girl who was in your room before you. (Laughs some more) She watched the beautiful valley way back there so long, she suddenly up and ran away. (Pause) Back to where she started. (Pim stops her slow walking and turns, stares at Nanny)

Pim — (Stared hard) She went back - to where she started?

Jerry — (Uneasy a bit) It happens once in a while. Don't let it bother you. (Sweeps an arm around) It doesn't bother us. (Nods away and leans back, closes his eyes) We're all going on to the bridge. (Yawns largely) Some day.

Nanny — (Sighs and looks toward the valley) Yes, that's right. (Sighs) I think so.

Beth — (Hand out) Come along, dear. We'll get you nicely settled down.

The key word - down - does not escape Pim's notice. Gradually, the temptations present themselves in the increasingly immense disparity between the comfortable, complacent, easy lifestyles of the others, and the tough, challenging, transient lifestyle of Pim's calling. Fortunately for Pim, she can see, as in "STRAIGHT AND NARROW PLUS", the disparity of the results of those lifestyles; the languid, dulled willfully ignorant and patronizing air of the others, compared to the vivid, joyous, seasoned and strong emanations of those seriously on the path.

Many paths exist, each with their own demands. Through Pim's example, we can see that, for those who are called by the Lord, there are no short cuts to faith in the task. Persons in Ministry are persons called, commissioned and, above all, EQUIPPED for the struggle - not against people, but against complacency, and the slow subtle slide to destruction.

Through viewing this particular Pilgrim's "progress", we are reminded that struggle is the Lord's tool, not to be avoided nor sought for itself, but a special part of the honor of God's unique call on our lives.

Chapter 11

DEALING WITH ESCHATOLOGY

Man will die. This is an unavoidable fact, however we may seek to obscure our concentration or notice thereof. But beyond the fact of our own personal death, is the fact that there will also be an end of time itself. The Bible states that there will come a time when our deeds and omissions are counted up, a balance made, and the results made available to our clear view. Whatever imagery we use to describe this Final Judgment, it is an inescapable fact, and for some, this fact more than anything else provides the catalyst to consider God's plan of salvation.

As with the other concepts dealt with thus far, communicative drama gives us various options when dealing with eschatology. One challenge to effective communication here is presented by the tones and timbres of many such communications made most recently. There is a tendency on the part of many to deal with the end of existence in a threatening manner - a kind of "THIS is what will happen to YOU if you don't..." attitude.

The pitfall inherent in such an approach is in its very nature. A threat implies control of the means of threatening. I cannot threaten anyone with that which I cannot control. Nor is it possible to achieve the results of faith by use of threats. In this sense, then, the "Judgment Day" cannot be used as a means to coerce anyone to faith. Faith is borne of love, not of fear.

Still, speak of the Judgment we must, so that no one may be allowed to fool themselves into thinking that reconciliation to their Creator can or should be delayed, put off until some vague "tomorrow".

Taking up the Challenge

Charles Tanner has undertaken this delicate task in his play, "THE LAST CHANCE". The setting of the play is a not-too-distant future, in which the Earth faces a destructive collapse of its continental plates. The seismic indications of the oncoming cataclysm have been interpreted by a group of experts, led by a Dr. John, and a "Metamorphic Panel" has been formed to prepare a mass escape plan, to save as much of the human race as possible.

For this purpose, massive spaceships have been built and are being kept in constant readiness all over the world. Access to these ships is free, and their staffs are chosen and trained on-board. The general populace has been fully informed about the ships and their purpose. Only one fact has been kept secret: that, when the critical seismic factor has been reached, and the launch program has been set in motion, a newly-designed force-field will be activated, to prevent those outside from storming and possibly destroying the ships, and thereby Humanity's only chance of survival.

"THE LAST CHANCE" takes place on one such rescue ship, upon which Dr. John has taken personal command. He is convinced that the critical factor will be reached soon, perhaps within a few days, but since he has no material proof of this, he can do little beyond issuing a warning, and continuing the necessary preparations.

In the meantime, he and his staff - Jess, Deam and Sheera, must deal with the prevailing problem of short attention span. As time progresses, and the immediacy of the threat diminishes, concentration begins to wander. Deam herself even finds it difficult to remain constantly in preparation, and begins to give her doubts freer rein. Finally, against Jess' advice, Deam decides to spend a night off the ship, convinced that one night won't make any difference:

Deam — I am going to have a night out. (Defiantly) And you can't stop me.

Jess — I know that, too. Guaranteed by the regulations. You know, the ones you'll be breaking.

Deam — That's my business.

Jess — (A sidelong look) What about Sheera? She's here only because of you. How do you think - this will effect her?

Deam — (Without being convinced of this) It won't bother her. (Short pause) Why should it? She does what she does and I do what I do.

Jess	That is not exactly what you told her to get her to come here.
Deam	She's a big girl now. She can handle herself.
Jess	(Quietly) You hope.
Deam	(Not happily) I don't want to talk about it anymore. (Firmly) I'm leaving tonight and that's all there is to it.
Jess	(Going to her, takes her by the shoulders) You will be careful, Deam? (A pause and a wistful smile) You are important to me, you know.
Deam	(Shrugging out of his grasp) Of course I will be careful. (Pause) I'm always careful. (Picks up some papers and heads for the door. Turns back, mocking smile) Don't leave without me. (He smiles at her - a bit sadly and says nothing. She exits and he goes back to work pensively)

Deam leaves, as yet unclear exactly when she will return, but determined to come back to the ship soon. Unfortunately, her decision is made for her, as before she can return, the critical factor is indicated, and the escape must begin:

Dr. John	(Quietly into the mike) All ship inter-com. The target has been reached. Abort test. Begin actual escape procedure. Interlock compartment bulwarks. Begin fuel prefrictionizing. Establish outer-wall –
Jess	Sir. Deam is outside!
Dr. John	(Evenly, but a bit sadly, too) Yes. I suspect others are too. Too many others.
Jess	But Deam is Cadre, sir.

Dr. John (To him) I know that, too. But we have reached the target line. Catastrophe is upon us. We do not know how long we have to accomplish lift off. Escape. We must begin now.

Sheera It's all my fault. I would not listen to you.

Jess No. It's no one's fault. The regulations are voluntary. It's up to each individual to keep them - or ignore them - or – break them. No one can follow them for anyone else.

Dr. John (Deeply sad here) Yes. Deam made her choice. (Into mike) Establish outer-wall integrity. Close all gates. Lock all doors. Solidify compartments. Lock all methods of egress. Liftlock in 77 seconds. (Sits and sighs heavily)

Sheera (Cries quietly but deeply) It IS my fault. Maybe I could have said something that would have kept her here.

Jess (Shakes his head) I'm afraid not. She was determined to go. I tried. She would pay no attention to me.

Dr. John (Feeling the loss of all, not just Deam) There was no way to convince them they did not have all the time in the world.

Jess She meant to come back. I KNOW that.

Dr. John (Nods) Most of them do. Some actually make it back, most do not. It gets put off.

Sheera If only I had done something.

Jess (Sighs) Yes. I know what you mean. If only I had done - MORE.

Dr. John (Sighs gently) If only I had said things - differently. Better somehow. Whatever words would have been convincing.

The thought has been advanced that this play exemplifies the ministry of Covenant Players itself. But truly, "THE LAST CHANCE" can exemplify any ministry; any group or work dedicated to the task of spreading the good news of Man's salvation to a world consciously seeking to avoid hearing of it. We may see, through Dr. John and those around him, the deep conviction which inspires the servant of the Gospel - a conviction that helps to overcome the frustrations that so often will come in the course of that service.

It is for this reason that "THE LAST CHANCE" has served to impact not only the "normal churchgoer", but those in active ministry as well:

"The play you did really was full of symbolism. I hope that everyone was paying attention about the points of the church and the 'unit system'. Everyone was so intrigued."

"I really enjoyed your performance. There was a guy who accepted Christ this morning at the prayer breakfast, who was at your performance last night. It was wonderful to see how the Lord lines those up. He went to the Bible study, your performance, and then he accepted Christ at the prayer breakfast. There was also a couple that haven't been to church in a long time that came last night, and loved it. I hope they were convicted, but those plays, especially ("THE LAST CHANCE"), are full of conviction. I mean, it not only refers to the Christian who goes out completely and commits carnal sin, but also to the Christian who just strayed but is still saved. She (Deam) knew the facts but she didn't really believe it."

"It may be futuristic, but its message is Gospel for today."

"It seemed to me that the play was causing me to look back and see where I failed to do something, or failed to make a difference in someone's life."

For Deam, as for those on the rescue ship, it is too late to change their determinations, or to return in time and change their words and actions. But this play - indeed all similar plays that take us beyond that amorphic “point of no return” - are not written for the characters in them, but for us; those who view them. We still have the opportunity to change, to commit ourselves to truly serve Jesus as He calls us to serve Him. We need not wait to wish for a second chance, as the rich man of Luke 16:19 - 31. We may, if we wish to see and accept, grasp the chance offered us today:

“Today, if you hear His voice, do not harden your hearts...” (Psalm 95:7, 8 NIV)

Chapter 12

THE LITTLE DESK AT HEAVEN'S GATE

Learning to Listen

I was once told by a man, while discussing the commandment concerning the Sabbath, 'When I stand before the Lord, and He asks me if I kept His Commandments, I don't want to have to tell him: 'All but one'." At the time I agreed with him, but after thinking about it for a time, it began to dawn on me that such a statement still misses the mark. To imply that we have only broken one Commandment would seem, to me, to be the height of arrogance. There is, in fact, only one answer when the Lord asks us, "Have you kept my Commandments?" That is: "No, Lord, not one."

Now, in all fairness, I don't believe that the man who uttered that pretentious-sounding statement can be accused of arrogance. In fact, I am certain, had he listened to his words at the time, that he himself would have qualified what he said. The point is, we do not always listen to our own words. And when we ignore our words, we ignore our attitudes as well.

To understand our attitudes, we must listen to ourselves, to the words that those attitudes engender. We must hear clearly the words we use, about the Lord, about our faith, about our neighbors, about ourselves. We must listen, too, with the proper sense of perspective in our minds. We must listen to ourselves as the Lord would, and will, listen to us; free from our own predispositions and rationales.

The vicarious quality of drama is aptly suited for this challenging task, and in the forefront of plays along these lines is Charles Tanner's "Registrar Series".

Defining Belief

The premiere play of the Registrar Series was "TRANSIT GLORIA", a play which, since it was written in 1972, has been translated in numerous languages, and performed in all parts of the world. It depicts a kind of office, one which is quite simple in its furnishings. There is only a small desk and two chairs, one of which is inhabited by a young woman.

Into this office comes Bob Sinclair, a man who has just passed through “a kind of gate”. As far as he can perceive, he is dead, and he is surprised to find himself in surroundings much different from what he had expected. He is even more surprised when the young woman mentions that she has a questionnaire for him to fill out, about his beliefs:

Bob — How many are there?

Registrar — Just five.

Bob — That doesn’t sound so bad. I ought to be able to handle that many. Toss me some easy ones, will you? Do I get multiple choice?

Reg — This isn’t exactly a school exam, Mr. Sinclair. It’s to find out what you believe.

Bob — Oh, well, why didn’t you say so? That should be a snap. I certainly should know what I believe, right?

Reg — Yes, you should.

Bob — Fire away, then. You get better accommodations with a good mark?

Reg — This is - quite serious, Mr. Sinclair.

In fact, Bob does have difficulty taking his situation very seriously, particularly since the questions seem too general to have much personal application to him:

Reg — The first question is about the Bible.

Bob — The Bible? That’s easy. I believe the whole thing, cover to cover.

Reg — As what?

Bob Well - as - the Bible, of course.

Reg 'What is it?

In trying to formulate his beliefs about the Bible, Bob identifies it as a book of rules. Logically, then, the next questions concern whether or not he has followed these rules. Here, both Bob and we discover an interesting fact: far from having held himself to these "rules", Bob is not even sure what all of them are:

Reg Could you name them, please?

Bob Name them?

Reg Yes.

Bob All of them?

Reg If you please.

Bob Whew! Well, there's that love your God one... and Thou shalt not steal ... Thou shalt not kill and thou shalt not covet ... Thou shalt not - lie ... and well - you know.

Reg That's five.

Bob I know. I could name them all, but it'd take time to think them out. And I got a lot of other things on my mind just now.

As the questions progress - the five major questions as well as secondary questions to aid clarity - Bob begins to identify that he has, in fact, very little knowledge or understanding of just what the Christian faith entails. He does have a philosophy, though:

> "Life's mighty complicated on earth. I believe the Lord takes that into consideration. But if you live a decent life, that should do it...

"You keep asking me questions about things that everyone - Christians, that is - believe in. I say I believe, and you want to know why. I don't know why. I don't think many other people do, either. Except ministers, of course, but then that's their business."

"Jesus died to save us from our sins. And I've lived a decent life, if I do say so myself. I went to church - pretty regularly. Gave as much money as the next guy - more than most maybe. I worked in the church - quite a bit. Kept the Commandments as well as most. And followed the teachings of Jesus - more or less."

"The basic things about Christianity - I didn't study them. I just believed them."

"I'm no saint, but I honestly feel that I deserve salvation as much as most church members. I worked as hard as I had time to."

Bob is particularly concerned by the focus that seems to be placed upon knowing what he believes.

Bob But I believe in everything. I do believe in everything. Even the Garden of Eden and Jonah, if you want.

Reg It's not what I want, Mr. Sinclair.

Bob But I believed in everything.

Reg Mr. Sinclair, belief isn't simply saying the words, "I believe." Belief is knowledge and practice. Many men have said the words, "I believe", but belied the fact in the living of their lives. People who are too busy to study the things that their lips say are central in life, are not believers. People who are too busy to learn about God are too busy to know God. Christianity is for the kitchen, the shop, the store, the garage, the factory, the living and working rooms of life; not locked up in the parlor for holiday viewing only. The Bible, likewise, is to be used, read, studied, worn,

> written in and wrestled with - not to decorate an isolated spot on a shelf, in dusty quarantine. The chief of the Commandments, you were told, was to love the Lord your God with all your strength, all your heart, all your soul, all your mind, and your neighbor as yourself. Heart, strength, soul, mind; the whole of man. To believe is to seek to know. To believe is to commit oneself completely. To believe is to dedicate one's being wholly to God. (A pause, then slowly) What do you believe, Mr. Sinclair?

This passage, known amongst the Covenant Players as the "Registrar's Speech", is one of the most concise and incisive explanations of the ramifications of a personal relationship with Jesus Christ in our time. Heard within the framework of Bob Sinclair's lifetime of habitual ignorance, of both his Savior and his calling, the Registrar's words are both convicting and uplifting. Her final question is as much for us as it is for Bob: 'What do you believe?"

Moments of Insight

The central question 'What do you believe?" forms the basis of the entire Registrar Series, a highly unusual series in the aspect that the characters differ completely from play to play. In subsequent plays, we see the wide spectrum of philosophies, creeds and standards of measurement represented in the various "applicants" to this office. For this is an office in the slight space between the World and Eternity. The gates we have passed are the gates of Mortality, and Judgment lies yet before us.

This is an important point, for the Registrar is not a Judge. There is no possible way to depict what is truly too intimate to remotely imagine, namely, the ultimate point at which we meet our Creator face to face. The purpose of the Registrar is to aid the applicant's vision.

It is for this reason that the Registrar changes from play to play. Each individual that approaches must be treated according to his or her individual understandings and misunderstandings.

In a sense, we see in each Registrar a reflection of the applicant to whom he or she is speaking. Some, like Bob Sinclair, need a series of questions to help the properly formulate their beliefs. Others, such as Andrew Peter Fisher in "NOT BY ME", need very little help to express the basic statements of their faith, but need to be helped to see that they do indeed believe. Still others, such as confirmed atheist Aldous O'Hare Russel, must first be acquainted with and brought to see the reality of their situation.

The answers to the questions placed by each Registrar have been as myriad and varied as the questions themselves. Audiences all over the world have borne witness to deep effect of the Registrar Series:

"I would like to thank the Covenant Players for coming this morning. They have shown us the basics in Biblical truths. That we as people just can't believe in something, but we should know why we believe it. I know that I am going to have to re-evaluate what I believe. Surprisingly enough for me, I was answering those things almost the same way that (Bob Sinclair) was. I know that in the future when I say 'I believe', I'm going to know what and why."

"I think the silence at the end (of the play) was because everyone was stunned."

"You know, as you were talking to (Bob Sinclair), asking so many questions, especially about salvation and what it means to believe, I felt as if you were talking to me. I congratulate your ministry. I'd like to study in a seminary when I finish high school - to be a pastor. Tonight your ministry encouraged me and strengthened me." (Buenos Aires, Argentina)

"That play was very mighty. It was heavy. I am a Christian and I know Jesus, but I have all these other things to do and I see how it has often been easy to let other things in my daily life become the important things and not Jesus Christ. I really need to remember and make Him always the most important. Some of the questions he had to answer I found myself very spoken to." (Hannover, Germany)

"That was good. Real good. Yes, I like it very much, especially (Transit Gloria). But tell me, where was he going when he went out that door?" (Covenant Player: Where do you think?) 'Well, I think he was going to Purgatory." (CPer: Do you think where he was going was the point of the play?) "Oh, no." (CPer: What do you think is the point of the play?) 'Well, it's about what you believe and how to have

faith every day. That's really hard ... well, it does give you a lot to think about." (Abbeville, France)

"There are two points that I understood. The first is about our focus in worship. We can come to church with the wrong focus. We must sing to God, worship God and take it into our daily work lives. The other is that belief is more than saying the right words at church, but our belief is to be practiced in the kitchen and the factory, places where we are every day of the week." (Bangalore, India)

"A few people, one or two, came up to me and said they were glad for it. But what I think is more important is to see that the people, as they were coming out of the church, were happy and smiling and hearty. They were talking to each other. They were not at all close in (to themselves). When they came to coffee afterwards, they were talking and laughing and jolly. I think we should take that as a sign." (Esbjerg, Denmark)

"Let it not be another play, another scene in life, but if there is something to change, do so - with the strength of the Holy Spirit – in your life." (Lemoyne, Pennsylvania)

"The argument between Jesus and Nicodemus is the same as the argument between these two people (in the play). We must all come before the judgment seat one day. And this man said, 'I was too busy, always involved in my prayers, went to church every Sunday... gave tithes and offerings, therefore I was qualified, because every time I could be found in the pastor's annals ... 'But listen, my friends, it is not the qualification. We are all going to Heaven because of Jesus, and the precious blood of Calvary!" (Kisii, Kenya)

An Alternate View

The effect of such plays on those who profess to believe in Jesus are telling, but even more telling are the reactions of those who actively disbelieve. As previously stated, disbelief must be maintained, and the stronger the touch on the conscience, the stronger must be the rejection of that touch.

Following a performance of "TRANSIT GLORIA" in Wroclaw, Poland, the performers were approached by a young man who introduced himself with the words, "Hello, my name is J., and I am an atheist and a Communist." He had not planned to attend the performance, but having done so, he could not help but speak with the team. His words reflect the power of what he had seen:

"Don't ask me what I thought about your plays unless you are ready to really hear." (CPer: Please tell us) "The first two plays were good. They were intellectual and made you think. But the last one ("TRANSIT GLORIA") was horrible. It goes against all common rules of conversation. The Registrar just sat there and asked questions about deep things, wrote down the answers. She didn't have to participate in the answering of any questions herself, or say who she was. She said, 'It's not what I believe', and 'the records are sent on'. Then she sent him on to a place they both had no idea where it was."

In subsequent conversation, he likened the Registrar to the Nazis in the concentrations camps during WWII - a very strong comparison to say the least. Too strong to be born of indifference.

This is perhaps the strongest evidence of the Lord's hand at work though the medium of Communicative Drama. This young man refused, in theory, to accept the existence of a Judge or the reality of a final judgment. Yet he could not help being both disturbed and challenged by his own identification with Bob Sinclair. In a sense, despite his own denial, this man stood in Bob Sinclair's place, and could not deny the reality of the judgment he had made of himself.

In 1 Corinthians, Paul writes "Now we see through a glass darkly, but then we shall see face to face". Common imagery induces us to anticipate a flashing view of our entire life before our eyes at the moment of our passage from this world. Yet, perhaps there is, in the split second between death the ultimate encounter with our loving Creator, an office prepared for each of us, be it simply or grandly designed, outfitted with computer or merely with the simplest writing implements, where we may hear ourselves in the unmistakable, unqualified air of true reality. And, as we stand convicted by the tremendous discrepancy between our words of faith and service and our deeds of self-centeredness, vindictiveness and destruction, we may hold on to words of comfort similar to those of the Registrar to applicant Norman Buckley in the play "NOT TOO RELIGIOUS"

Norman (Starts off [through the audience], his legs wobbling a bit and his pace that of a funeral procession, head down. He gets about halfway or two-thirds of the way down and stops, looks ahead with fear and something of horror and then turns toward the Registrar, a muffled cry) I can't face Him. (Voice breaks at the end, but very slowly he starts on down) I have no defense.

Registrar (With sorrow and compassion and yet hope in her voice, speaks - which he may or may not hear, as he continues to move along) Remember - your defense sits at His right hand.

www.ingramcontent.com/pod-product-compliance
Ingram Content Group UK Ltd.
Pitfield, Milton Keynes, MK11 3LW, UK
UKHW041920190726
13854UKWH00003B/1352